In loving memory of Alicia Haley, my American Mom
I Loved you then, now, and always!

And for my sons, Dillon and Deven
Eu Te Amo!

Shirley was the fastest girl in school. The annual Turkey Trot was just a week away and everyone knew that Shirley would be bringing home the first-place prize, a big, fat, frozen turkey. Shirley had legs that looked like stilts; one of her strides was equal to five of mine.

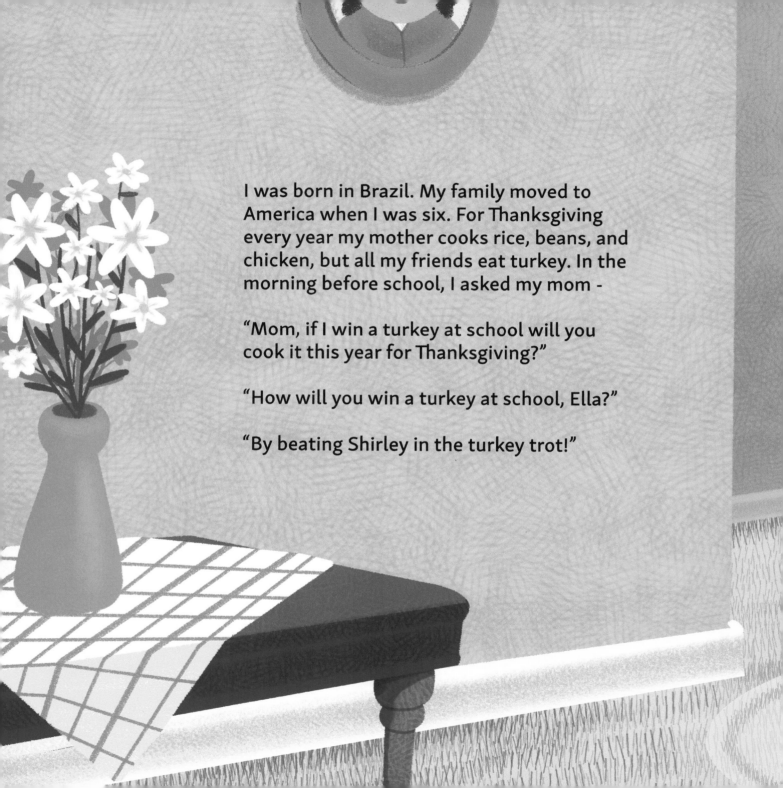

I was born in Brazil. My family moved to America when I was six. For Thanksgiving every year my mother cooks rice, beans, and chicken, but all my friends eat turkey. In the morning before school, I asked my mom -

"Mom, if I win a turkey at school will you cook it this year for Thanksgiving?"

"How will you win a turkey at school, Ella?"

"By beating Shirley in the turkey trot!"

The day had come. My whole fourth grade class was lined up at the starting line. We had to run one lap around the school and then it was a straight shot to the finish line. Shirley was to my right.

The big, fat, frozen turkey sat on a picnic table to my left. I eyeballed the turkey good and hard for a moment before I took the runner's stance.

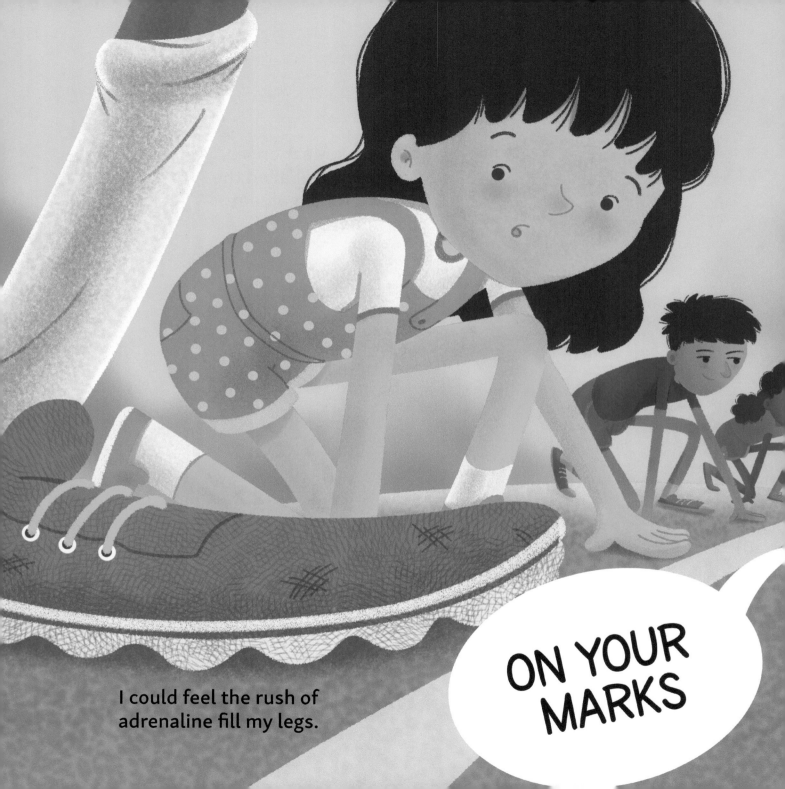

My heart is beating uncontrollably fast while the image of a golden roasted turkey faded into the distance.

I threw my body forward with all the strength I could muster, and within a few steps I had taken the lead over the whole class. But as expected, I felt the sleeve of Shirley's tee-shirt rub against my arm as she moved in on me. We were neck to neck, but I still had the lead by a hair and there was no way I was letting her pass me.

I made my way around the last corner of the school building and now it was a straight shot to the finish line. The whole school was watching. The one strap from my polka dotted jean over-all came undone and was flapping freely in the wind. Shirley was still breathing her hot breath down my neck and then it happened…

I CROSSED THE FINISH LINE...

I placed the big, fat, frozen turkey
on my lap during the bus ride home.
As the bus approached the
apartment complex a rush of
contentment came over me.

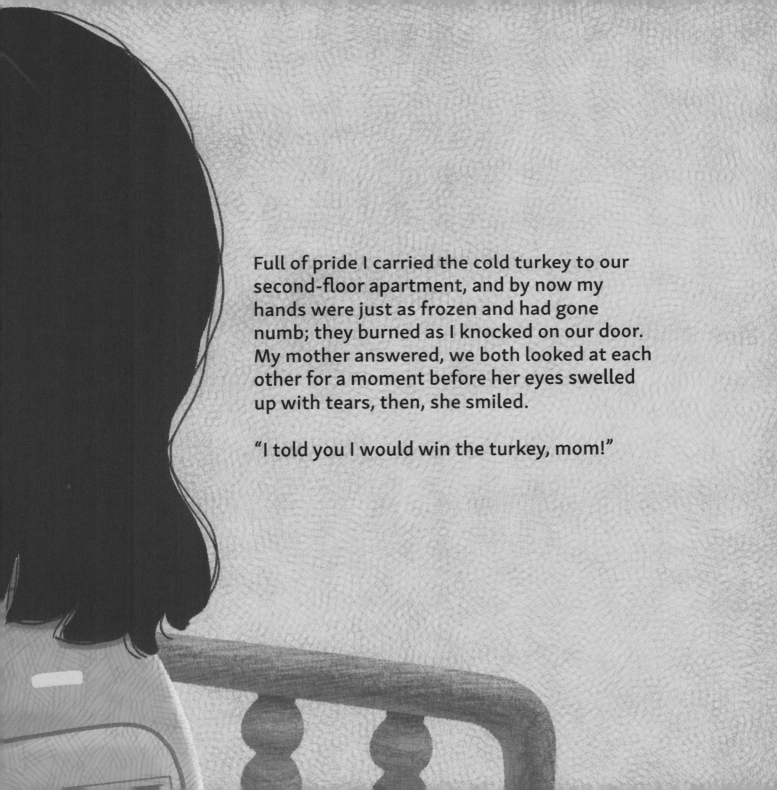

Full of pride I carried the cold turkey to our second-floor apartment, and by now my hands were just as frozen and had gone numb; they burned as I knocked on our door. My mother answered, we both looked at each other for a moment before her eyes swelled up with tears, then, she smiled.

"I told you I would win the turkey, mom!"

That year for Thanksgiving and every other that followed, we had rice, beans... and turkey.

A Brazilian native, Rafaella was born a storyteller. She moved to the United States with her family at the age of six. Her writing is a mixture of coming-of-age in America with deep ties to her Brazilian roots.

From a young age, Rafaella thrived when given the freedom to be creative and explore her vivid imagination — from writing to photography. Her passion is bringing readers on a memorable journey filled with laughter, some good tears, and a whole lot of heart.

Leandro Francisca has worked as a graphic designer for magazine and book publishers, but his great passion has always been drawing. In 2018 he was invited to illustrate his first children's book - Musical Circus - The Story of Tião. This was the turning point in his career. While working on this project he discovered that illustrating children's books was a better use of his talents.

Printed in the USA
CPSIA information can be obtained
at www.ICGtesting.com
LVHW061119251123
764913LV00015B/75